Amelia Earhart

Women

From the very first days of powered flight, women were determined to be more than just spectators. They were eager to experience the thrill of flying. They wanted to become pilots.

Throughout the tough, exciting years of early aviation, many women pilots risked their lives, and some died.

Along the way they created and broke many records, undertook flights of great daring, and became legends in the history of aviation.

Amelia Earhart was one of these legendary pilots. She believed that women could do anything, and she set out to prove it.

Therese Peltier – first woman airplane passenger

Aviators

Amelia Earhart

1908

Early Life

Amelia is born in 1897... She is an adventurous girl... Her family moves from place to place... At twenty, she moves to Toronto and becomes a nurses' aid... She sees planes up close for the first time.

Amelia Earhart was born in Kansas in 1897. From the very beginning, she was a fiercely independent girl – adventurous and athletic.

Amelia's father worked for the railroad. The family never settled in one place for very long before he was moved to a new job in a new town.

In later years, Amelia was to comment that because she moved around so much as a child, as an adult, she could never stay in one place for very long.

Raymonde de Laroche – first woman to hold a pilot's license

4

A young Amelia (left) with her family in Kansas

1910

During the winter of 1917–1918, Amelia visited her sister in Toronto, Canada. World War I was raging in Europe, and in Toronto, Amelia saw many wounded soldiers.

Amelia was so deeply shocked by the sight, that she enrolled in a first aid course. She worked as a nurses' aid in a hospital until the war ended.

While in Toronto, Amelia visited an airfield. It was winter, the snow was thick on the ground, and the planes' propellers churned biting ice into her face. She could almost feel the sensation of weightlessness as she imagined herself lifted into the air. She decided then and there that one day she would ride one of those "machines."

Harriet Quimby – first American woman to hold a pilot's license

Amelia studied
medicine at
Columbia
University.

1911

LOS ANGELES, CALIFORNIA, 1920

Amelia moves to Los Angeles, where she takes her first plane flight... She decides to take flying lessons... To pay, she works at a telephone company, sells sausages, and drives a truck.

Amelia and her flight instruct

Feeling restless after the war, Amelia eventually moved to Los Angeles, the center of America's growing aircraft industry.

Hilda Hewlett – first British woman to hold a pilot's license

Anita "Neta" Snook

There she took her first flight. She paid ten dollars for a ten-minute joyride over the city. As soon as she left the ground, she knew that she wanted to fly a plane herself.

Amelia had heard of a woman pilot who gave flying lessons, and in December 1920, she became a student pilot with Anita Snook.

1911

9

A Dangerc

In 1928, Amelia flies as a passenger on an epic transatlantic flight... First they lose their way... Amelia is soon a star.

In April 1928, Amelia was asked if she would like to become the first woman to fly as a passenger nonstop across the Atlantic, with veteran pilots Wilmer Stultz and Louis Gordon.

Amelia agreed to go, welcoming the chance for an adventure.

Secrecy surrounded the flight for fear that publicity might lead to a race for the record. Amelia couldn't even tell her parents what she was going to do. She left them notes, which she jokingly referred to as "popping-off letters," to be delivered in the event of a crash.

Harriet Quimby – first woman pilot to cross the English Channel

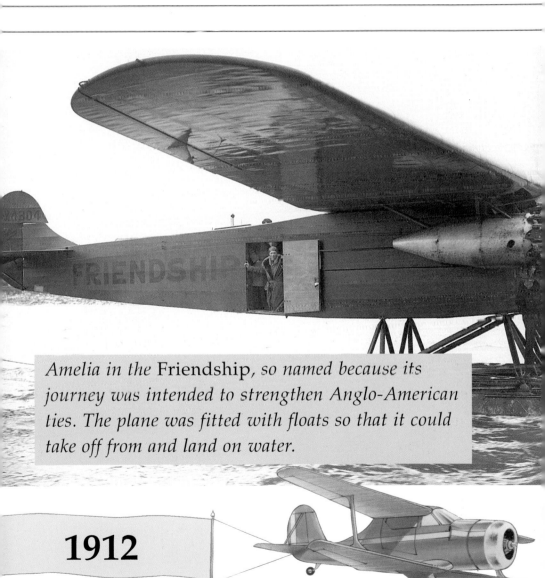

Amelia in the **Friendship**, *so named because its journey was intended to strengthen Anglo-American ties. The plane was fitted with floats so that it could take off from and land on water.*

1912

11

Amelia spent the long and troubled flight huddled in the aircraft's tiny cabin.

They flew through thick clouds for most of the trip, and had to rely on instruments to get their bearings. The radio broke down early on in the trip, making it impossible to keep a check on their position.

After flying for nineteen hours, and with only one hour's fuel left, the aviators were unsure how far they were from land.

During a break in the clouds, they saw an ocean liner. Amelia dropped a message in a bag, asking for directions to be painted on the ship's deck. The bag missed!

Katherine Stinson – first woman to loop-the-loop

A safe and successful landing: The Friendship *reaches its destination at Southampton. The danger surrounding long-distance flights was great. In 1927, nineteen people died while trying to fly across the Atlantic.*

1915

Much to their relief, the crew spotted the coast and landed the plane in Wales. The flight had taken twenty hours and forty minutes.

Upon arrival, Amelia was a star. She was the first woman who had ever dared to make a transatlantic flight. Embarrassed by the publicity, Amelia said, "All I did was lie on my tummy and take pictures of the clouds!"

She soon put her new-found fame to good use, however, speaking out about the contribution women could make to the future of aviation.

Ruth Law – breaks cross-country record flying from Chicago to New York

President Calvin
Coolidge wired Amelia
a congratulations on her
transatlantic crossing.
She wired back:
*"SUCCESS ENTIRELY
DUE GREAT SKILL
OF MR. STULTZ."*

1916

A Wome

In 1929, Amelia takes part in America's first women's derby…

Within a year of Amelia's transatlantic flight, America staged its first women's air race. Amelia took part, along with twenty other women.

The women's derby was more than just a race. It was a grueling cross-country adventure covering more than 2,800 miles. The women flew from dawn until dusk for nine days. They flew over mountaintops and across stretches of desert, with little more than compasses and road maps to guide them. Of the twenty pilots who started the race, fifteen finished. Amelia came in third.

Katherine Stinson – first woman pilot to tour China and Japan

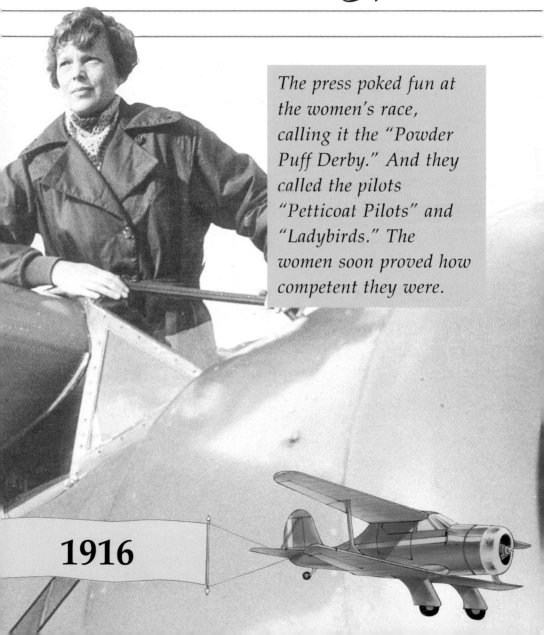

ı's Derby

The press poked fun at the women's race, calling it the "Powder Puff Derby." And they called the pilots "Petticoat Pilots" and "Ladybirds." The women soon proved how competent they were.

1916

Solo

In 1932, Amelia flies solo across the Atlantic... She is now a true celebrity.

After the derby, Amelia decided that she was going to fly the Atlantic again – only this time she would fly by herself.

On May 20, 1932, Amelia took off alone from Newfoundland.

She headed out over the Atlantic Ocean, bound for Paris. It was to prove a dangerous and eventful flight.

Soon after departing, Amelia realized that her altimeter reading was incorrect. With darkness falling and a faulty height-recording instrument, she was unsure how high above the waves she was.

Bessie Coleman – first African-American woman to hold a pilot's license

18

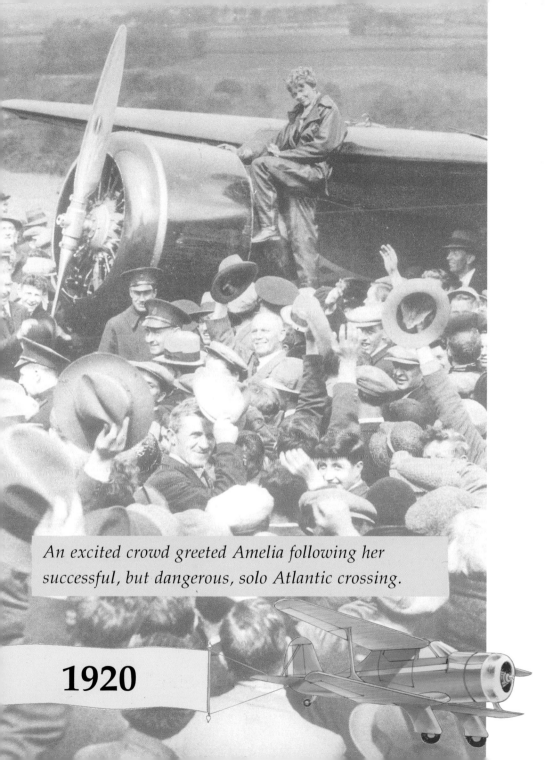

An excited crowd greeted Amelia following her successful, but dangerous, solo Atlantic crossing.

1920

By midnight, Amelia was flying through a fierce thunderstorm. She tried to fly above the storm, but ice formed on the wings and forced her to descend. Suddenly, the plane went into a wild spin. She struggled with the controls, righting the plane just above the jagged whitecaps shimmering in the darkness.

With the approaching daylight, Amelia could see flames forcing their way through a crack in the plane's exhaust system.

When she checked the plane's fuel tanks, Amelia discovered that a line leading to the fuel gauge was leaking. This meant that Amelia had to find land, and soon.

Amy Johnson – first woman to fly solo from Britain to Australia

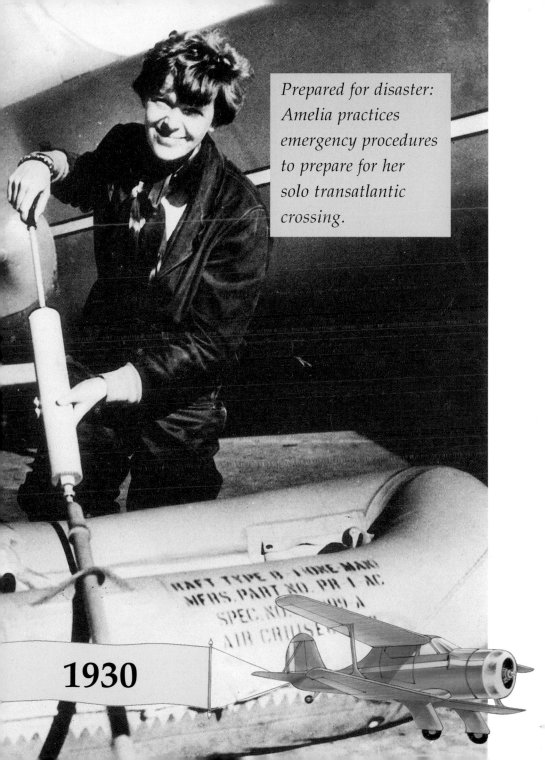

Prepared for disaster: Amelia practices emergency procedures to prepare for her solo transatlantic crossing.

1930

Finally Amelia saw the coastline. She landed in a field amid a herd of cows. An astonished farmer told her that she was near Londonderry, Ireland. Amelia simply said, "I've come from America."

Amelia had succeeded in her quest to fly solo across the Atlantic. The flight set a new record for the fastest crossing at fifteen hours and eighteen minutes.

Ruth Nichols – sets new women's altitude record

For her transatlantic flight, Amelia received honors in both Europe and America. This time she was famous as an aviator in her own right.

1931

Lucky

LUCKY CHARM
BRACELET

SILK
SCARF – AMELIA'S TRADEMARK

POWDER COMPACT

A melia liked to travel light, even on long flights. On her solo flight across the Atlantic, the only food she took with her was a thermos of soup and a can of tomato juice. Her emergency kit took up most of the space.

Other aviators packed lots of food and even fancy clothes.

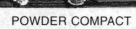

Jean Batten – first woman to fly solo from Britain to Brazil

Charm

When Lady Heath flew across Africa in 1928, she took with her a selection of tennis rackets, six gowns, and a fur coat!

One thing Amelia always took with her, however, was her lucky charm. This charm was a bracelet inlaid with silver. She forgot it on her last flight.

IN-FLIGHT FOOD

STAY-AWAKE SMELLING SALTS

EMERGENCY LIGHT

1935

Record

In 1932, Amelia sets a transcontinental record...
In 1935, she makes the first solo flight across the Pacific...
Later, she flies from the United States to Mexico and back...
She plans to fly around the world.

A melia wasn't home for long, before she was in the air, breaking records again.

Beryl Markham – first woman to fly Atlantic solo from east to west

Breaker

In 1932, she set a new solo record for a woman pilot on a nonstop transcontinental flight from Los Angeles to New Jersey. Within a year she repeated the journey, cutting two hours off her record time.

In 1935, she became the first pilot, man or woman, to accomplish a solo flight across the Pacific Ocean from Hawaii to California. This was a greater distance than the transatlantic flight.

1936

Lengthy alliance: Amelia shown here with Allan Lockheed in front of the Lockheed Vega in which Amelia made her record-breaking flight across the Atlantic.

Jean Batten – fastest solo flight from Britain to New Zealand

T hree months later, she was off again, flying solo nonstop from Los Angeles to Mexico City, then from Mexico City to New Jersey. She was the only woman to make this north to south, south to north flight.

They were all remarkable flights, but Amelia felt that there was one more great journey left for her to make – she wanted to fly around the world.

At about this time, Purdue University set up a research fund, which enabled Amelia to buy a Lockheed Electra, a plane capable of making a flight around the world.

1936

U.S.A., 1937

The Lockheed Electra is readied for the trip... Fred Noonan is signed on as navigator... The first attempt to set off around the world ends in disaster.

The Lockheed Electra was the fastest, most advanced aircraft of its time. It was a powerful, twin-engine plane.

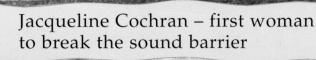

Jacqueline Cochran – first woman to break the sound barrier

It could reach speeds of more than 200 miles per hour.

The plane was specially prepared for its epic journey. The ten passenger seats were taken out and replaced with long-range fuel tanks. The cockpit was fitted with up-to-the-minute instruments.

1953

Amelia wanted to make the flight on her own, but for such a long and involved trip, she would need a navigator. She signed on Fred Noonan, a transport pilot and navigator of great experience.

Valentina Tereshkova – first woman in space

Amelia's first attempt to fly around the world ended in disaster. On the journey's second leg, the plane was flipped over on takeoff by a gust of wind. The aviators were unhurt, but the plane was damaged. It had to be rebuilt, and the trip was delayed.

1963

A Secon

Amelia makes a second attempt to fly around the world... They take the longest and toughest route... They make many stops along the way.

On May 21, 1937, Amelia Earhart and Fred Noonan took off from Oakland, California.

They were headed for Miami, Florida. It was the first leg of their eastward journey around the world.

On June 1, they were airborne again, this time bound for Puerto Rico, then flying in easy stages down the South American coast to Brazil.

Jerrie Mock – first woman to fly solo around the world

Attempt

Ready for the second around-the-world attempt, Amelia stands with husband, George Putnam, in front of the rebuilt Lockheed Electra.

1964

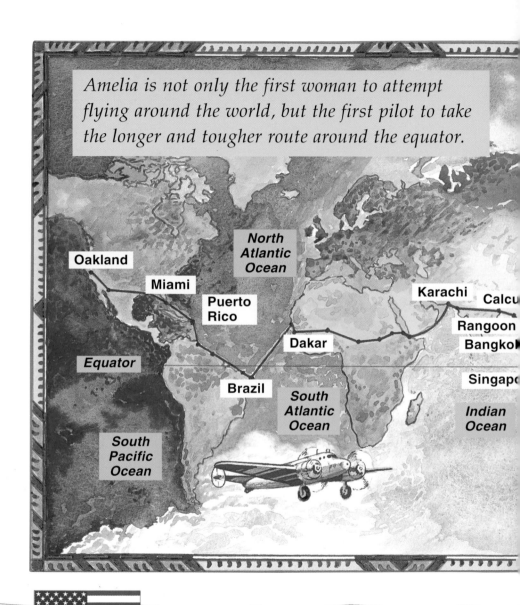

Amelia is not only the first woman to attempt flying around the world, but the first pilot to take the longer and tougher route around the equator.

Oakland

Miami

Puerto Rico

North Atlantic Ocean

Karachi

Calcu

Rangoon

Dakar

Bangkok

Equator

Brazil

South Atlantic Ocean

Singapo

Indian Ocean

South Pacific Ocean

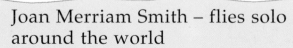

Joan Merriam Smith – flies solo around the world

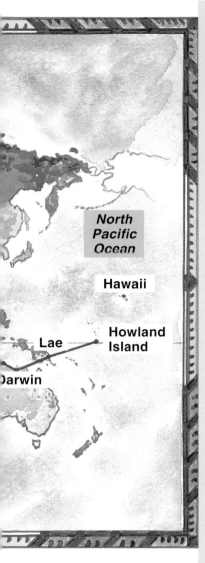

North
Pacific
Ocean

Hawaii

Lae

Howland
Island

Darwin

1964

On June 7, they left South America and headed out across the Atlantic Ocean to Dakar, on the west coast of Africa. From there they flew over Pakistan, India, Burma, Thailand, Singapore, and Darwin to arrive in Lae, New Guinea.

At prearranged stops along the way, Amelia's name was painted in huge letters on waiting fuel drums. The letters became a welcome sight to the weary travelers. Though the stopovers meant a needed rest, there was little time for sightseeing.

In Amelia's last dispatch, from Lae, New Guinea, she wrote, "I wish we could stay here peacefully for a time and see something of this strange land." Nearly the entire Earth had passed beneath their wings, yet the aviators had seen only a kaleidoscope of colors slipping by.

Once they reached Lae, they had covered more than 22,000 miles and had only 7,000 miles to go. This was the most difficult stage of the journey. It involved flying over the Pacific Ocean in search of a tiny coral island called Howland Island, their last refueling stop before Hawaii and home.

Sheila Scott – first British woman to fly solo around the world

Named the Flying Laboratory, *Amelia's Lockheed Electra was well equipped for aerial research as Amelia attempted her epic flight.*

1966

The aviators head for Howland Island... They have trouble finding their way and run dangerously low on fuel... A full-scale search is launched.

A t 10 A.M. on July 2, 1937, Amelia Earhart and Fred Noonan boarded their plane at Lae. Both were tired from the constant traveling and Amelia was ill.

Sheila Scott – first solo flight in a light plane over the North Pole

For this final and most dangerous stage of the trip, they had taken everything that wasn't needed out of the plane – even their personal gear. The fuel tanks were so full, the plane could barely lift off the jungle runway.

The flying time to Howland Island was approximately twenty hours. Estimated time of arrival was 6:30 A.M. The U.S. Navy had positioned the coastguard cutter *Itasca* off Howland Island to help Amelia with directions.

1971

In a series of radio communications with *Itasca*, Amelia said she was flying through heavy clouds, and was unsure of her exact location. In a later call she said they were running low on fuel. Her last call came in at 8:45 A.M., and she sounded strained. Amelia Earhart was never heard from or seen again.

A massive sea and air search was launched to look for the aviators. It was hoped they would be found afloat in a life raft or marooned on an island. President Franklin D. Roosevelt ordered a dozen ships to search the area. The search lasted weeks, but nothing was ever found.

Amelia's mother anxiously awaits news.

Jeana Yeager and Dick Rutan – first nonstop flight around the world

THE WEATHER

Saturday and Sunday generally fair and warmer

Columbus Evening Dispatch

OHIO'S GREATEST HOME DAILY

VOL. 67, NO. 3. • • • Telephone—MAin 1234

SATURDAY, JULY 3, 1937.

14 PAGES

Wirephotos
Associated Press
International
News Service

PRICE

AMELIA'S VOICE, CALLING S-O-S, IS HEARD BY LOS ANGELES RADIO MAN; SIGNALS SPUR SEARCH

FLYER'S OWN STORY WRITTEN BEFORE LAST TAKEOFF

By Amelia Earhart

Operator Sure He Heard Flyer

Planes and Ships Rush to Hunt For Aviatrix, Down at Sea After Futile Attempt to Reach Howland Island.

Where Earhart Is Lost!

CUTTER SEARCHING HERE FOR FLYERS

BAKER I.
40 MILES SOUTH OF HOWLAND I. WHERE EARHART MAY HAVE LANDED.

Such a Tiny Island

FRED NOONAN

MISS EARHART JOKE

Port Columbus Attached That Amelia Is 'One of

Famed Flyer Has 'Dropped In' at Airfi Times; Cranter Recalls First Meeting

Clipper Ship On Transatlantic Hop

Woman Windo

Smasher So

Noonan Noted Among Flyers

Around the world, newspapers ran front-page headlines, such as "The Pacific Claims Earhart." All sorts of stories grew up around the disappearance of the adventurous aviator.

1986

43

U.S.A., AMELIA LIVES ON

Amelia Earhart had been a daring aviator, adventurer, and an inspiration to other women. She had encouraged women's interest in aviation and given them goals to strive toward.

Amelia wrote in a note just before her death: "Women must try to do things as men have tried. When they fail, their failings must be a challenge to others." After Amelia's death, other women aviators took up the challenge with equal courage and determination.

Julie Gibson – first woman to graduate as a pilot in the Royal Air Force

1991

Index

From the Author

Amelia Earhart was an adventurer, and her story is one of courage and daring.

I have always enjoyed reading the stories of explorers and adventurers, especially those adventurers who set out to do what people said could not be done.

I hope you enjoy the story of Amelia Earhart, and that it inspires you to read other books about people who have made amazing journeys.

David Lowe

LITERACY TREE

What Courage!

Written by **David Lowe**
Illustrated by **Bryan Pollard** and **Ray Downham** (aircraft timeline)
Photography by **Hulton Getty Picture Collection:** (pp. 11-13;
p. 15; pp. 20-21; Amelia Earhart landing at Culmore, pp. 22-23;
pp. 32-33; pp. 40-41; Amelia Earhart's mother, p. 42; pp. 44-45); **Photobank
Image Library:** (cover, p. 3; p. 7; pp. 14-15; pp. 17-19; Amelia Earhart
after solo flight across the Atlantic, pp. 22-23; pp. 26-31; p. 35; pp. 38-39;
newspaper article, p. 43); **Schlesinger Library, Radcliffe College:** (p. 5;
pp. 8-9)

05 04 03 02 01 00
10 9 8 7 6 5 4 3

Published in the United States by

Rigby

a division of Reed Elsevier Inc.
500 Coventry Lane
Crystal Lake, IL 60014

Printed in Hong Kong
ISBN: 0-7901-1859-9